THE STORY OF

Ford
Thunderbirds

by David K. Wright

Gareth Stevens Publishing
A WORLD ALMANAC EDUCATION GROUP COMPANY

Please visit our web site at: www.garethstevens.com
For a free color catalog describing Gareth Stevens Publishing's
list of high-quality books and multimedia programs,
call 1-800-542-2595 (USA) or 1-800-387-3178 (Canada).
Gareth Stevens Publishing's fax: (414) 332-3567.

Library of Congress Cataloging-in-Publication Data

Wright, David K.
    The story of Ford Thunderbirds / by David K. Wright.
       p. cm. — (Classic cars: an imagination library series)
    Includes bibliographical references and index.
    Summary: Surveys the history of the Ford Thunderbird and its designs,
engines, and performance.
    ISBN 0-8368-3191-8 (lib. bdg.)
    1. Thunderbird automobile—History—Juvenile literature. [1. Thunderbird
automobile—History.] I. Title.
TL215.T46W75 2002
629.222'2—dc21   2002070577

First published in 2002 by
Gareth Stevens Publishing
A World Almanac Education Group Company
330 West Olive Street, Suite 100
Milwaukee, WI 53212 USA

Text: David K. Wright
Cover design and page layout: Scott M. Krall
Series editor: Jim Mezzanotte
Picture Researcher: Diane Laska-Swanke

Photo credits: Cover, pp. 5, 7, 9, 11, 17, 21 © Ron Kimball; p. 13 © Isaac Hernández/MercuryPress.com;
p. 15 Courtesy of the Detroit Public Library, National Automotive History Collection; p. 19 © MercuryPress.com

Printed in the United States of America

1 2 3 4 5 6 7 8 9 06 05 04 03 02

*Front cover: In the 1950s, many people
dreamed of driving a 'T-Bird' convertible,
such as this 1956 model.*

TABLE OF CONTENTS

Words that appear in the glossary are printed in **boldface** type the first time they occur in the text.

CRASH PROJECT

The people who ran the Ford Motor company were upset. The year was 1953, and Chevrolet had just introduced the Corvette, a two-seat sports car. Chevrolet was part of General Motors, Ford's big **rival**. Ford needed to make a sports car, too! The company had always made fast cars, but now it had to make a fast car that also looked sporty.

Corvettes had smooth curves, so Ford created a car with sharper edges. It was low and stylish, and it had only two seats, just like the Corvette. Ford called this new sports car the Thunderbird, after a **mythical** bird from a Native American **legend**.

In the 1950s, Ford came out with a racy new car called the Thunderbird. This red Thunderbird is from 1955, the year the car was introduced.

A POWERFUL SPORTS CAR

Ford began selling Thunderbirds in 1955. Right away, "T-Birds" got a lot of attention from people. They were just as pretty as Corvettes, and they came in more colors. One model had a top with a **porthole** on each side. With room for just two people and a powerful V-8 engine under the hood, the Thunderbird was a true sports car.

Ford and General Motors copied each other. Ford copied the idea of making a sports car, but General Motors copied the idea of using a V-8 engine. Ford had been putting big V-8 engines in its cars long before the Thunderbird. The car was a mix of old and new ideas.

When Thunderbirds came out, they were a big hit! These models are all two-seat convertibles from the 1950s, but they are each slightly different.

ADDING PASSENGERS

Two-seat Thunderbirds were very popular, but not everybody was satisfied with the car. Some buyers wanted a car that could carry more than two people and had more room in the trunk. After only three years, Ford stopped making the two-seat Thunderbird.

The 1958 Thunderbird was a new, much larger car. It could carry four people, and it had room in its trunk for several suitcases. The car had fins in the back and razor-sharp lines, but it was no longer a sports car. Thunderbirds now **appealed** more to older drivers and to people with families.

By 1958, the Thunderbird had become larger so it could carry more than two people. This 1959 Thunderbird convertible has long fins in the back!

POWERFUL T-BIRDS

Thunderbirds were no longer small sports cars. The cars were still fast, however, and many people began to use them in **stock car** races. Race drivers knew that the engines in Ford Thunderbirds were big and powerful. They **modified** the Thunderbirds, turning them into race cars!

These racing T-Birds only had one seat, and they also had a special roll cage that would protect the driver in case of an accident. The cars were much louder than normal Thunderbirds, because their V-8 engines did not have mufflers. The cars ran on big **oval** racetracks. Although they started out as regular T-Birds, they were much faster!

This 1963 Thunderbird is for everyday driving, but it has a powerful engine. In the 1960s, some people turned T-Birds into racing cars!

LONGER AND WIDER

In the 1960s, Thunderbirds kept growing. They were now large, **luxurious** cars. Customers could buy a **convertible** model, but they could also buy a four-door **sedan**. Ford made other cars that cost more, but people bought Thunderbirds because the cars looked expensive — and fast.

By 1967, Ford no longer made a convertible model of the Thunderbird. The front of the car now looked like a jet plane, and it also had hidden headlights. When a driver turned them on, the lights popped out from behind little doors!

A Thunderbird from the 1960s is a long, wide car! This 1965 T-Bird was used in the 1991 film Thelma & Louise.

THE BIGGEST THUNDERBIRD

The 1976 Thunderbird was the biggest ever! It weighed over 4,500 pounds (2,040 kilograms). At the time, gasoline had become very expensive. Many people had stopped buying big cars because the cars used too much gasoline. They drove smaller cars that used less gas.

In 1977, the Thunderbird shrank! The new car was a foot shorter than the 1976 model and weighed much less, too. Ford soon offered this new, smaller car only as a two-door model. Besides being smaller, this new Thunderbird was very luxurious.

Although this 1976 Thunderbird was a huge, heavy car, only two people could sit in it comfortably. The 1977 Thunderbird was a much smaller car.

THE "AERO" LOOK

In 1983, Ford introduced an exciting, all-new Thunderbird. It was a sleek and pretty two-door coupe. People said this new Thunderbird had an "**aero**" look, because it had the smooth shape of an airplane.

Ford offered the new model with a choice of three engines. Besides the larger V-8, buyers could choose a smaller V-6. Buyers could also choose a four-cylinder engine that came with a **turbocharger**. Turbochargers were often used on race cars. With this special engine, the new Thunderbird flew down the highway!

In the 1980s, Ford made Thunderbirds that looked much different than earlier models. This 1986 Thunderbird has a turbocharger for extra power.

A SAFER CAR

Ford made many improvements to the Thunderbird in the 1990s. The company added better brakes so the car would stop more quickly and designed an engine that created less **pollution**. Thunderbirds also grew in size. Ford designed new **suspension** so the cars handled and rode very well.

Although these Thunderbirds were good cars, Ford had trouble selling them. Maybe they looked too much like other cars. The company stopped making Thunderbirds after 1997, and rumors began to spread. Was Ford planning to build an all-new Thunderbird?

By the 1990s, Thunderbirds had come a long way from the early models. This red 1995 Thunderbird is parked next to a 1955 T-Bird.

THE THUNDERBIRD REBORN

In 2001, Ford introduced a new Thunderbird. This new Thunderbird looked a lot like the first model that came out in the 1950s! It was a small two-seater, and it was available as a convertible. The new car even had a hardtop with portholes!

The latest Thunderbird is a mix of the old and the new. Beneath the surface, it has many modern **innovations**. On the outside, however, the car has much of the style of the classic Thunderbird from the 1950s. Like styles of clothing or music, car styles may go out of fashion, but they come back again!

The T-Bird has returned! This 2002 Thunderbird is a fast, modern car, but it definitely has a "retro" look that reminds people of a car from the 1950s.

MORE TO READ AND VIEW

Books (Nonfiction) *T-Bird: 45 Years of Thunder.* John Gunnell and Ron Kowalke
  (Krause Publications)
T-Birds. Doug Mitchel (Metro Books)
Thunderbird 2002. Michael Lamm (Motorbooks International)
Thunderbird Milestones. Enthusiast Color Series. Mike Mueller
  (Motorbooks International)

Videos (Nonfiction) *Driving Passion: America's Love Affair with the Car,
  Part 3 — Golden Age of Detroit.* (Turner Home Entertainment)
The Visual History of Cars: Thunderbird. (MPI Home Video)
The Visual History of Cars, Volume One. (MPI Home Video)

PLACES TO WRITE AND VISIT

Here are three places to contact for more information:

Auto World Car Museum
Business Route 54
Fulton, MO 65251
USA
1-573-642-2080

**Henry Ford Museum
& Greenfield Village**
20900 Oakwood Blvd.
Dearborn, MI 48124
USA
1-313-271-1620
www.hfmgv.org

National Automobile Museum
10 Lake Street South
Reno, NV 89501
USA
1-775-333-9300
**www.automuseum.org/
info.html**

WEB SITES

Web sites change frequently, but we believe the following web sites are going to last. You can also use good search engines, such as **Yahooligans!** [www.yahooligans.com] or **Google** [www.google.com], to find more information about Ford Thunderbirds. Here are some keywords to help you: *classic cars, Ford, T-Bird, Thunderbird,* and *vintage cars.*

www.autoclassics.com/tcn/gallery/gallery.htm
Gallery of Featured Thunderbirds has many color photos of classic Ford Thunderbirds from the 1950s.

www.fordheritage.com/tbird/
The Ford Motor Company hosts this web site. Learn about the history of the Thunderbird and get listings of Thunderbird clubs.

www.fordvehicles.com/cars/thunderbird/index.asp?model=true
This is the official Ford Thunderbird web site. At this site, learn all about the latest Ford Thunderbird models.

www.geocities.com/MotorCity/Show/4232/Thunderbirds.htm
This site has a brief history of the Ford Thunderbird. It is easy to read and has pictures of the different models made through the years.

www.omniport.net/alinodot/mybird.html
The person who hosts this site has a 1957 Ford Thunderbird. Visit this site to see pictures of the car.

www.tbird.org
This site has a lot of photos, and it also has a T-Bird of the month.

www.tbirdranch.com
The person who hosts this web site has a yard full of old Thunderbirds! The site has a lot of pictures and information.

GLOSSARY

You can find these words on the pages listed. Reading a word in a sentence helps you understand it even better.

aero (AIR-oh) — having to do with airplanes and flight 16

appealed (uh-PEE-uld) — attracted interest 8

convertible (con-VERT-uh-bull) — a car with a top that can be folded back or removed 2, 6, 8, 12, 20

innovations (in-oh-VAY-shunz) — new inventions or ways of doing things 20

legend (LEDGE-und) — a historical story passed down through the years that is usually part truth and part fiction 4

luxurious (jen-er-RAY-shun) — providing a lot of comfort and pleasure 12, 14

modified (MOD-if-eyed) — made certain changes to something 10

mythical (MITH-ih-cull) — imaginary 4

oval (OH-vull) — egg-shaped 10

pollution (puh-LOU-shun) — waste products that are harmful to the environment 18

porthole (PORT-hole) — a small, round window that is often found on boats 6, 20

rival (RY-vul) — a person or group that competes with another person or group 4

sedans (seh-DANZ) — large, enclosed cars that can hold a lot of people 12

stock cars (STOK cars) — racing cars that are based on everyday passenger cars 10

suspension (suh-SPEN-shun) — the system that keeps a car steady over bumps 18

turbocharger (TUR-boe-char-gur) — a device that gives an engine more power 16

INDEX